Black Hollyhock, First Light

Black Hollyhock, First Light

❋

Judyth Hill

LA ALAMEDA PRESS :: ALBUQUERQUE

For my father,
Edward Schwartz, of blessed memory

Praise & Gratitude to– Dolores LaChapelle, Martín Prechtel,
Robert Bly, Gioia Timpanelli, Jeff Bryan, Joan Logghe, Art Goodtimes,
Nancy Schmitz, Lee Schwartz, and Rockmirth. And John. And Rockmirth.

Cover art: Joseph Biggert
Black Hollyhocks Too – oil on linen

Frontispiece: Joseph Biggert
Black Hollyhocks #1 – oil on linen

Bio page photograph by the author
of *The Little Bear Who Trashed Our House*

ISBN # ↗ 1-888809-23-x

Library of Congress No. ↗ 00-133124

La Alameda Press
9636 Guadalupe Trail NW
Albuquerque, New Mexico 87114

table

Preface

"Japanese poetry has its seeds in the human heart and burgeons into many different kinds of leaves of words. We who live in this world are constantly affected by different experiences, and we express our thoughts in words, in terms of what we have seen and heard. When we hear the warbler that sings among the blossoms or the voice of the frog that lives in the water, we may ask ourselves, which of all the creatures of the world does not sing? Poetry moves without effort heaven and earth, stirs the invisible gods and demons to pity, makes sweet the ties between men and women, and brings comfort to the fierce heart of the warrior."

Tsurayuki,
from the Preface to the *Kokinshu*,
(compiled in 905 A.D.)

Inspired by my book, *Sacred Land*, Talking Gourd is a small community of poets and poetry lovers who meet in the wild and form a ritual space for poetry that deeply addresses experience of place.

Here, many years ago, I met Judyth Hill.

Judyth Hill and sculptor John Townley, live in a ponderosa pine forested canyon between Mora and Las Vegas, New Mexico. On the steep north face of the canyon, they have built a unique homestead called Rockmirth, a combination art farm and 100 acre stewardship of natural habitat and extensive garden beds.

Following the life of the flowers through the seasons and the shifting light of the sun as it plays upon the mountains, Hill's poetry is influenced by the essentials of Chinese and Japanese poetry. In her poems, we actually experience the *notan* of great Japanese paintings – the gleam of the wet black against luminous mists – and always changing.

In the old form of Chinese characters, *yang* is represented by the sun with its rays, together with the character *fu*, meaning hill or mountain. The character for *yin*, was a coiled cloud along with the character *fu*, while *yang* describes the sunny side of the mountain, and *yin*, the side in shadow.

This relates directly to the changing relationship of the sun and the mountain. In the morning, when the sun is behind the mountain, the trees are dark, almost black, in the afternoon when the sun shines directly on these same trees, they are bright and glowing with light.

Ernest Fenollosa, the great thinker on Chinese art and poetry, wrote that the "contrast of light and dark is inconceivably splendid." This alternating light and dark in Hill's poetry leads us into the real relationship of the human at home in the natural world. In her poems we experience the ancient *yin-yang*. We are not stuck in one mood, or one way of thinking.

Sorrow, in Hill's oeuvre, shifts swiftly into joy.

In her poem, "We Attain Incessantly the World to Come," she refers to "Hollyhocks laddering open . . . " this closely observed moment moves us through the seasons of both nature and our lives.

As George Orwell said, "The versifier tells us what we already know but says it better than it has been said before; the poet shows things we have never seen."

Judyth Hill is profoundly a poet.

Dolores LaChapelle
Silverton, Colorado

Step outside onto the Planet
Draw a circle a hundred feet round

Inside the circle are
300 things nobody understands, and, maybe
nobody's ever really seen

How many can you find?

O

LEW WELCH

Heart's Clarion

Soft haired pasque flowers,
Poke through pine needles.

Each year, first blossoms to appear on the mountain.

Noticing them, in an afternoon lit,
Then stormy. A tendriled cowl,
Framing the delicate lavender petals,
Surrounding the many-sepaled inside.
Scented, surely, for bee love.

Bloom within bloom,
Like the way we contain more than we contain.

(The possible cradling the impossible)

They're everywhere, you said.
Just like that.

Quite Contrary

Small patch, stitched by lavender, scented by tarragon
You're greening up!
I come often to your wakening edge, these days
Of March's odd and earnest advancement.

You are greening up:
Minty shoots brave the bluster, the crazy transient hail
Of March's odd and earnest advancement.
I too, am coming I hope forward.

Minted shoots face the bluster, the here again gone again storm
Not to be outshone by the bravery of greens,
I vow to begin again fresh.
As red clay learns by compost, the yielding ways of loam.

Not to be outshone by the bravery of greens,
I too long to start over:
As clay surrenders to what must and will grow,
Break open, give way to not known seedling.

Written Wet

What part of the truth is always dark?
Today I found the soft place beneath the rough bark of cottonwood.
Like the innerness we long for, it is wet.

Exposed to our hidden moisture,
We too begin to leaf out.
In the canopy, leaves flicker in a downpour of light.

Groping, we scribble and scribble.
Leaves cast dappled shade, a pattern similar to remorse.
At the edge, the values meet.

Scribbling, we grope towards truth.
Light wears a skin of darkness.
Cottonwoods, a skin of light.

Heaven and Earth

Tulips have a short lifespan, like happiness
they unfurled into April, blatant, oral,
and luscious. Smooth crimson cups with a schmear of dark.

Opening in morning, the petals curling back by noon.
For once I remember to go and look, thinking Heaven and Earth,
and that the Chinese and Lakota call Heaven, "Blue Sky."

Volunteer mulleins crowd the day lilies, the ones John poached
from up the canyon, the ones we'll see flower, first time,
this year, like us, transplants gone native.

This beauty of a life, dirty dishes in the sink and the phone all day
but delirious by way of bulb and rhizome:
It's what's underneath that counts here, counts for everything.

If the Season Fits, Wear It

Spring arrived in tatters,
skirt of snow,

mudboots, string of pearls,
sleeveless,
but still somehow decorous.

One tulip flamed,
then another. Narcissus making plans,
mint aromatic, but not hastily.

Slowly, we recognize desire.

Patiently, shedding outer skins.

Piercing the curded soil, a tender shoot, greenling,
everything we have ever cultivated by hoe or spade.
Tools intend the flower.

Turn the earth, think the thought.
Wait.

Chinese Sorrowing

I love to paint women,
and the woman I love to paint most is myself – Frida Kahlo

Ravens fly East, towards Spring.
Mournful, all day the late snow fell.
Cold, in my cold bed,
I wonder how it is with you.

Harsh wind from the North
sends unseasonable storms
up the canyon.
Settles on the Rociada ridge.

Likely the pass has closed, and much has happened
too sad to speak of this night.
Chrysanthemum tea gone cold in the cup.
Grape hyacinth blanketed over in drift.

Plum Wine in March

I turn away.
Return alone, to a lonely bed.
A rain black as the crow night, only the fragrance
of lilacs rises to the window, and the wisteria
dangles on the painted trellis.
Wrapped in a quilted cover, in a pattern of Wedding Rings,
I gesture from sleep, my hair loosed from bands.
The porch beckons, the taut railing
and damp cherry trees, their small pink fists.
Venus rises in the southern heavens,
the Twins wheel recklessly overhead.
This is not a night for sleep.
There might almost be cranes,
the confluence of brooks in the distance.

This Night, Different from All Others

A scourging wind today, and tonight, many prayers.
The blessings for light, and kiddush sung over wine.

Blessing bitter herbs, and stories:

Moses' barefoot on holy ground, his temper,
his stutter, family stuff: his sister Miriam, the part about bulrushes.
The part with ten plagues, ending in a night of bloodshed.

The next morning, miracle, a sea parts for slaves.

All this day, simmering my mother's perfect soup,
(The secret is cloves, and peppercorns, and grief.)

Her good dishes, her death, the table set with stories:

My temper, my sister Nancy, the part about rosebushes,
the part with a recipe for salmon, why the parsley,

who left whom, and who is set free,

on this night, by remembering.

More and Less, by Noonlight

First hummer heard, rush to fill feeders.
A primary day: blue sky, red insistence,
flock of goldfinch.

From these, comes the possible.

Come colors, all spin and whistle,
frogs in the pond, largesse of moon.

From this fullness, again, empty.

Work, and the heart's lifting,

weeding, and clearing of weeds,
the pleasures of a tended bed.

And the turning over that is so like singing,

and sugar water, only really sugar water, for sweetness.

A wild wind scours through,
that music, the true honey.

Temper Mental

Those tulips have finally caved.
Snow and simply, time
have wicked their effervescence.

Next, we'll trim their dimmed green,
turn the earth nearby,
and seed the early ones.

Peas, and tender romaine, Bloomsbury spinach,
radishes we'll neglect to harvest, will sprout,
come to leaf and fruit. If not careful,
we can dream them all the way to compost.

Garden Party

Planted peas.

Three kinds of lettuce, lechuga,
Corn early and late, sunflowers to go with.
Some dill. Left space for radishes.

Left space for spinach & cilantro, longstanding:
Said to withstand heat. They all do, or don't.
Withstand heat, that is.

I make rows, as seams.
Then zip them closed, 1/4 inch under, if lucky.

The dead are all around us, breathing on our seeds.

When planting, I feel them, a hand on my shoulder,
A suggestion. But my ancestors weren't gardeners!

Their advice, confusing, odd: Read Ovid. Wear a hat.
Study Lucretius. Write your sister.

Stop with the romaine and buttercrunch, already.

Listen to us, listen, then water.

Waking in the City of Holy Faith

You have to believe in something here.
Blue skies and early willows say so.
And delicate apricot in bloom.

You have to believe this fruit will be gathered,
dried, or painstakingly brewed into jam.
Or eaten out of hand or pocket.

This is a town about fallen fruit, like most.
Fruit on roadsides, in gutters, come late July,
fruit in moist, rotting glut in thick buffalo grass.

But you have to believe in that too.
That's the trick.

A Matter of Individual Drops

You could have counted them, if you were there.
Instead, in some inner place, you were busy.
This breaks the rules of the road.

This breaks the heart of the world. It's a matter of attention.
A poet's job is to stay not busy.
That's the work, that's how you know what the weather is.

On this land, we're in the bird business.
Nuthatches scurrying up tree and down,
studious devotees of the skin of ponderosa.

I wish I knew the words for the pitched locomotion
of mourning doves, their earnest back and forthing
in the soft fallen needles. But I could show you,
if you had the time.

It's the mysterious logos of the wild.
The untranslatable heart of the utterly present.
But singable. Note by note, drop by drop.

Two Buddhas in Our Garden

One, where you've moved him.
The other, where, all last summer, he was.

Under Shandokah

Walking to where falling water makes four sounds.
We find a glade tuned to the truth in a pocket of pond.
It's the inner loom of forest, hung with webs and willows weft,
a fluff of seed and scatter.

Wild geranium vines up. The cinquefoil,
branches fallen in a harsher season.
Flax fixes us with wild blue eyes, a yellow iris.
Mouths filling with the lush body parts of flowers:

Umbels, stamens and panicles, a confusion, a profusion.
Is it gentian, or false hellebore?

Have I lost the line between penstemon and
scarlet gilia?
Lost my mind to monkshood and cow parnsip?

No! The names have been the way in:
brought me here beneath
the rubythroat's air show, all Eros and no telephones.

I make a call on the nested ones,
those who crest upon night.
Losing my way, I learn to wing it.

Begin, I say, with what you don't know.

When You are Receptacle, You Become Mule's Ears

in the rooted community. As in

aspens, a shudder and hiss,
the gray blue ceiling of flicker above
and beneath, cow parsnips umbrellizing over their leaves.

Warblers calling tree to tree.
vireo's nest on the ground, woodpecker's
picking insects from the sap in etched bark.

There are myriads of details. Not to mention
that algebraic relation between the breeze
and this coolness on my skin.

Everything here is lifting or maybe
dropping down. Similarly, osha is a great healer,
and water hemlock, poisonous. Also,

stroking nettle the right way,
they can be visited without sting.
Saturated with color, in the shade of the grove

the surrounding meadow reads brilliant green,
which otherwise would bleach out in sun. Our
eyes have become little camera obscura, click,

click, our notebooks full of questions.
Six separate shades of yellow
and they all have names.

We're nearing revelation: pattern
emerges into an affordance
of opportunity,

Telling it true, we stand
in the cool, damp glade,
absolutely phenomenal.

How Frogs Practice Silence

I wish I knew the determinate tone
That chooses, or selects, that sudden quiet.
How the chorus quits, en masse,
As if a leafy baton had fallen.

Is there a chord or, lilt, or lift of key,
That signifies to the pond community
A hush in unison.

I wish I knew when to be silent.

Could hear the moment before the saying,
And leave it so.

Then recommence in counterpoint,
A ratcheting, a rattling, a declension upscale
And down, but in place, and in tune,
With my fellows.

Walking the Field of Vision

These vegas aflush with color,
and us, awash in a sea of naming,
a field of many grasses.
Lush, succulent at the roots,
buffalo, fox tail, longspine sandbur,
an OED of meadow.

Clumps of pinky clover,
bees will plot on their map of sweetness.
What is the cartography of our sweetness?
My compass always whirling towards true North,
while I long to orient South,
to the place of pure grove.

Pressing on,
my steps disturb the soft turpentine musk of sage.
A scent that scours us towards wisdom.
Bending lower, I get personal with pentstemon,
their sullen bitten lips,
their twinned rapprochement on a single side of slender stalk.

Brain sees leaves, says lanceolate.
Sees light stopping at the vibratory rate called purple.
Brain will not let me off the cognitive hook.

I admit I am a slut for facts,
wantonly lusting for data.
Storing it away for a future of forgetting, asking, forgetting.

At least I'm not begging for the phylum, kingdom, species, speech.
I obviously have a genius for erasure.

My savannah's a blur of greens blowing hillward,
bowing to the place they lock into vertical.
Today, I too, am purposefully vertical
on Wilson mesa, watching a distant bough of aspen,
and walking, suddenly I see

the spaces inside landmark lengthen.
I see the between, where the deer run,
what elk see. Shifting light sweeps the smooth flank of hill
sheen then shade.

The stretch and release of landscape—
everything, I mean everything moving!
All these flowers doing their Hootchie Kootchie
C'm here baby, Oooh la la thing.

Set to cicada, the tuned being I'm becoming
sings all the way to sneeze.

A westerly wind whips through,
clearing language, swallowing voice.
The mind, in the on/off blare of lit aspen,
finally quiet, bows down.

Swoon of Seeing

Above, bright blue dragonfly skittering.

Under delectable skin of water
Such a depth of rippled cloud
Resting on the velvet, emerald moss.

As far away in the inner world
As love, or sorrow.

From Red Bank

I was formed by the pull of the Navesink River.
Staccato light through sycamores.

Seagulls went out to sea riverwise and returned.
Night and morning, then night. And that stipple of light again.
I tasted longing first in thick, salt air.
The scent of a seatown, the boardwalk. My father.

I have the inner geometry of slant.
I learned this from avenues leading to ocean,
a slope followed into dream.

I was formed by that downward inclination,
by a river in swift meander,
the song of bobolink and wren.

I was formed by snapping turtles,
nearly asleep in afternoon sun,
Temper and temperament, what soothes:
the holiness of naming.

I was formed by a storm that filled the river,
how she rose in her bed, and I in mine,
rose and rose and ran tumultuous down to the mineral Atlantic,
the way I know to disappear into the larger story,
enamored of the flavor of men and good water.
Buckets of steamers, broth and butter.

I was formed by wet weather and the fog weaving in,
by shifting light,
moon growing large bellied, to fingernail crescent
and back.

I was formed by what rushes towards us,
and what flows away,

by granite and pylons.
Broken by surf, by bay and inlet,
by pier and barnacle.

By obstacles that shine.
I was formed by poems in English,
by rhyme and meter and horizon
I was grown iambic, seduced by hexameter.

I sucked words from river mist,
and was formed
by the crack between rock and word,
moon and stone,
river bed and river.

The Mulberry Bush Wedding

We went round and round,
All the way, humming
buoyant, a man and a woman with no corners to turn,
rhyming to the calm surfaces of pond,
the clean sling of moonbeam.

We may or may not know circle,
are often confused by maps,
but trust the turning curves:
The way there,
will surely become the way back.

Mantras come in circles, also, hats.
Maybe marriage.
The number zero and the o of surprise.

I promised to be around, in the manner of nectarine,
of plum, which is to say,
certifiably lunar.

To start my melody, when you are two lines into yours.
To end on the same note.

My mouth watered,
thirsting for a cocktail of vodka and lightning,
cooled by the speckled shade of sycamores in full leaf.

I wish I could turn round,
see you here,
band on my finger.

We go to Hawaii,
we go again.
How many times do we need Paradise?

We go to India.
We go again.
How many glimpses of the Beloved?

We were married here.
On earth.
Hills spilling into chamisa,
Aspen. Trees whose zones
I am just now learning.

It's positively global, how everywhere
is on the way to this place.

Umpteen Blue Jays Later

Four balds and the baby goldens
we saw in the Bosque:
I was there, and watched you turn
exquisitely into the light, older.

A flock of red wing blackbirds overhead,
and it's later.
Twelve years, thirteen whoopers, sandhill cranes,
and conversations always stopped
by the swoop of redtail.

Many pine siskins later,
hooded junkos and the one time only oriole.
We're older. Maybe wiser,
but certainly richer in magpies and starlings.

And once, a rufus headed towhee.
Now 100 ravens roam our hillside,
dark enigmas of flock and scatter.
Remembering the sounds their wings make,
Listen darling, I say, they are playing our song.

And the doves with their soft call.
I'm calling too. Your name,
into the rich and common air,
Hieron, the space between.
That emptiness full of song and flight.
I'll meet you there.

Sonnet in Search of More Wisdom

For Oriental Poppy was invented the word crinkle.

Exactly to say the crush of rumple inside that fuzzed green cap
which splits to reveal the intricate bunch of tissue petals,

That relax, stretch out, into their silken life at the end of stem.

Then the smoothing out from a hidden beginning
that in no way predicts the festive.

I married that way.

Marriage is that same compression, how we're folded
frowzy bloom at the center of it's journey towards flower, seed
and whatever happens next.

But certainly relies on that crunched, scrunched encasement
to get there.

Wherever that is, flower bed, or marriage bed.
Let it be sweet.

Nocturnal Suite

She came to visit us in the night,
and admired the pillow cases,
hand-embroidered and crocheted by the Great Aunts.

I'm glad you've solved your linen crises, she told me.

Cream colored stitchery as done only in the long ago.

What's a Jewish girl doing with good Irish linen, I wonder,
as well, 4 cats or hawks overhead.

There's a subtle happiness
in the mysterious unfolding of gladiolus.
First the slim spears fan out,
develop a suggestive wrinkle, an itch of blossom.
Then a rounded shoot, etched, Oriental, emerges.
Exotic, erotic shoji flower, secreting
the ardent crimson interior.

We watched this salacious coming to bud and bloom,
haunted by the pursed red velvet of the petals.
Haunted too, by the mother,
sliding through dream,
sewn in the fine fabric of our common sleep.

Why Do Men Whistle?

Men whistle when they work.
Birds whistle while they are birds.
It's their job.
Good benefits, but rough hours.

No sick leave and they can't take holidays.
But do birds need vacations?
Not the six magpies in their green black iridescence
and noisy scolding. A chatter, a flutter, black, white, black.

A chess board in flight.
Not the red-tails, out of some inner darkness rising.
Hawks flick their wing-tips and hold,
in paired luminous cruise, a halo over canyons.

The way their attachments are always elsewhere.
Beyond households and calamity.
They pin nothing on refrigerators.
They are a postcard from the infinite.

Not the swallows in their urgent gathering,
a tour group, a bus load,
swoop and glide on the B plan, with continental breakfast.
Feeding is their beat,

they sing for their supper,
for the sheer joy of having a ticket to everywhere.
Not the eagle, the avian aristocracy,
that seer of the great distances,

his view is his vacation.
Or the red winged blackbirds, in their uniforms
of somber ecstasy, a squadron, spending it all
on a whim of scarlet.

But men, let's get back to them.
Men whistle when they are in tune,
because they don't need English for happiness.
Men making a house with other men

make dust, and decisions, and a joyful noise.
Raising struts and joists, they commit.
Say, I do, to trusses and 2x6's.
Create a new thesaurus entry under Shelter.

Men whistle to keep their spirits up,
and practice the shape of kissing.
Men put their lips together and blow,
to make music, that artifact of love.

Nacimiento, Neruda

If only your green eyes flecked with sun
did not buzz and hum all night
to the ragged shore of morning.

If only this mountain was not so much like the sea,
rising and falling on our breath,
and these hills, forgiving themselves over and over into valleys.

So much like the great foaming heart of the poet,
his sweetness a path through piney forest,
his metaphors like honey.

We sob and press, closer,
an intricate, edible presence,
melted tissue thin,
a membrane away from nectar.

Everything Aspires

Tufted ear squirrel at the feeder,
keeps cautious lookout, feasting on seed.
Then scampers off, startled
by some shift in the landscape I've missed.

I don't miss much these days.
I'm a tuning fork to the winds.

I want to tell you about this wind.

Temperatureless, vast.

It's blowing through our days
And we're becoming parabolic,
curved and crystalline as the pinnacles in Tent Rocks.

I mean everything in me that shines is showing.

I mean everything that came round to now
is asking for our touch.

I mean that we are standing in the only place we can stand.

Nothing holds here, but you and I and the wind.

Soon, even we will be gone.

That Fearful Symmetry

Between fire, water, air, earth, dances another:
Smoke is the fifth element.

The first puff appeared over the ridge around three.

Then plumes of black billowed as whole trees went up.

One canyon away.
Soon the ridge was crowned with flames.
Within minutes.

I was planting columbines. Rocky Mountain Blues.
There was nothing to do but pray.

I pleaded in every language, to every deity I know,
psalms for the chipmunks, sutras for the bears,
chants for underbrush, incantations for the redwing.

Lit a votive to the Guadalupe for the stands of pine.

I begged.

I called on Ameratsu, Quan Yin, Yemaya.

Offered deals,
what I'd give if the land was spared.
How better I'd become.

You would have too. Fire roaring one canyon over.

Wind whipping the blaze through stands of pine.
Helpless, watching.

Friends call, offer to get us out.
We try to decide how we could possibly leave,
what wouldn't it matter to keep.

Evacuation, and Then

Packing up paintings.

What books? Machado's *Times Alone*, Neruda's *Love Poems*,
Rumi, Eliot, Schwenck's *Sensitive Chaos*.

Pictures. The kids: ages baby to now,
Holding Cassidy's hand, his owl bottle.
His graduation, Amanda at every moment.
My mother, my mother,

What little left, so precious. Everything precious.

The rose bush, just bought,
Peace blossoms in bud.
Honeysuckle.
We finally this year found, where honeysuckle is happy.

No no no, can't pack, can't part with plant or plate or

say goodbye, at least in heart.

Have to know what matters is finally not matter,
but matter yes, also.

Joseph calls, says, for the land the fire is a bad haircut,
for you, well, we re-build.

I am looking at grandma's spoons,
at John's braid, when I cut his last brown hair.

Starlings have moved into our bedroom's corner eave.

I'm listening to that jazzy caroling of bells,
the babies make when fed.

I'm listening for what they know about nest.

All Day, the Bear

Seen at the hummingbird feeder this morning
is with me.

Against the bulk of that furred body,
the trivial is instantly clear.

It's deliciously hard to have opinions
and think of bear
looming on the mountainside.

All day, pulling Russian thistle and knapweed
against the wind
and the will

of what is larger,
and always prevails.

It Takes a Crisis to Make a Village

I'm sitting in my broken happy orchard,
A fistful of pencils in my hand.
Whatever happens,
I'm somewhat ready for it.

Lately, large brown bears amble down the mountain,
Lured by the siren's call
Of salmon on the grill.

Don't ever say, "There he is" around here—
Our nerves are completely shot.

Fire alerts,
Bears appearing like constellations,
And now a swarm of bees.

Idyllic and rural, that's us.

The corn is faring well, thank you.
Though my neighbor's didn't. Is that banal?

Are we a village yet?

With so much trouble in the canyon,
Everyone says hello, and discusses the weather.

Happiness makes for lovers, but woes make community.
We have friends that come by, and friends that stay away.
The kettle is on, bread's in the oven, all news is good news.

Fidelity, Mutual and Insurance

A Chase Manhattan lady assured me
that her extra coverage
would be additional to any I might carry.

Then told me she was sorry
not to have been able to protect me,
from cancer she meant,
for chemotherapy and my hospital stay,
supposing that I need these in my future.

Nothing weeps so well as a willow, I almost said,

since that was what I had been thinking when she called.

But I don't know her,
and perhaps that would have been an unfair answer,
aligning myself with trees in event of illness.

I said, I prayed to stay well, but failing that,
hoped not to respond with a medical experience.

She couldn't quite hear those words,
and so kept wishing me health,

and I was never able to tell her
we had just planted two peaches, and an ash.

Too Much with Us, Late and Soon

Lilies stupefy.
Midsummer too glorious,
Beauty beyond heretic capacity.

Towers of delphinium,
An overwhelm of blue.

Sunflowers, marathon, mums begun
Sweet peas about to, garden agog.

Isn't this so the way of glamour?

Rolling in and in, until we're gasping, saying

No breakfast thanks, I have seen the corn in tassel.

No lunch.
Nasturtiums seem about to bloom, Empress of India,
And I am preparing to be retinue.

Any day Peacock orchids,
will dazzle beside that imagined crimson.

And dinner?
Impossible, having seen the Stargazer.

Southern Fish in August Sky

Here the two worlds become one.
There is no choosing,
but the falling towards each other.

I am in your dreams.
You have dreamt of that soft wooden bridge
suspended low over the stream.
Remember the one we crossed in the wood's heart?

It hung deep into the water.
Japanese bells chime in the distance,
from the monastery that must be there.

Koi flickering by, coins of that realm.
Silken, golden as wishes, they glide by our legs.
We lie down there and then.

Ahh, Beloved,
Now we are in the two worlds!

The River of Already

*As I was among the exiles on the River Kevar,
the heavens opened and I saw visions of God* – Ezekiel 1:1

Picture that river, the reflection
predicting where the red-tail swerves.
Picture that view, where fences dissipate
into mere punctuation, making
a simple sentence of landscape.

Create the necessary syntax to say this.

Learn to spell freedom as ravens might,
translate over, as hummingbirds,
the feeders taken down, timely, in late August.

First frost, a fatal sweetness.

Finally, there is only those soft fallen grasses,
gone to burnt umber and some color we probably call dusk.

Impossible loves, dark as the curled petals
in the cold garden.

So many Stellar jays later.
The top of the ridge later, and finding true North.
What a suture of trails we'll need
to heal this shifting season.

Autumn sky, true blue, like nothing I can attest to,
never having seen forever, but something like it:

a blaze of last sun through old, old cottonwoods
in San Patricio.

Patrick,
patron of wayfarers.
And me, as ever, saying I do.
Marrying risk and never as easily as ever,

That's how I write this,
stars filling my pen.

Knowing it's just true.
And maybe the only truth I know.
A reflection.
A revelation.
Singing out, later, a crazy joy into pure blue dark.

Pine Sings, No Wind

Han Shan
(T'ang Dynasty, late 8th-9th centuries, A.D.)

Chamisa waves, not yet bloomed
But pricked with beginner's luck
I'm lucky too, in the way of out-breath

Tamarisk wave, not yet blooming
Lizards skitter across warm rock face
I'm lucky too, in the way of inbreath

Forgiving myself lightly, as if it were the first time

Lizards skitter across rim rock
There's no road but the road we're going anyway
I'm forgiving us both, as if it were the last time

As if there were song in the wind

We Attain Incessantly the World to Come

The way we recall raspberries
Is full on September, gladiolus
Finally unfastening, hollyhocks laddering open,
Fat bud by fat bud. The interminable suspense
Of mums is over. That waiting for flower.

Patience reminds us of winter's necessities:
Cedar in the stove, ashes to clear daily,
Taken to the compost box reserved in summer
For weeds and spent blooms.

Deep snow will pillow these ashes,
Take them, potash and all
In a hissing embrace.

There's nothing overt here,
Mostly nuance.
In winter we re-discover minutia.

Fine shadows of the pentstemon and millet
Over the white ground, etching of squirrel
Track and 'coon, trampling at the feeder
With starling and wren.

Most of the garden caught us lazy.
Fall splintered stalks, a tangle of down vines
Remain in endearing repose, stalwart, custodial.

Guarding the place of their next arousal.
History might arouse them,
But not politics.

Governments no,
But perhaps at some meeting, someone
Will raise their hand tentatively
And call for a vote of confidence
On the reliability of horticulture.

The motion will be seconded,
Coffee surreptitiously sipped,
Lapels fingered nervously,
Or ties. Sleeve cuffs pulled down
And straightened, as meetings
Turn their agendas
To the apparently undiminished,
Irrepressible constancy of seeds.

The Economics of Generosity

The sun rose and ravens flew,
Stellar jays on the amaranth:
bright blue on vermilion seed heads.

Golden light, luscious. This morning, my husband says,
To grow amaranth is a political act of unstinting beauty.

Last night, our neighbor's cow
in our garden again.

Open range here, our responsibility to fence them out.

Early Spring, the garden barely in,
I drove in my nightgown and a rampage down to Joe's,
howling that his cows were out, and on our land.

They'd eaten the young locust trees to bare branch,
we lost one.

Joe was sorry that day, said he'd try.

He has. 'Til the tell tale *Moo* at 3:00 am.
I was too tired to fling stones at cows or entreaties at Joe.

Autumn and exhaustion make me generous.
What corn we've left is dry on the stalk,
first frost has already taken the tomatoes.

I ponder neighbors, and fences and the few cosmos left,
crimsons and creams. Juncos and siskins
feasting on the heavy heads of sunflowers.

It's all of a piece. We're flush with honied light,
and the hustle of small feeders in spent beds.
In this season we are actually rich.

What is one fence less, one cow more?

Day of Two Snakes

Walked late.

Past a curve of copper colored oak,
a stand of Virginia Creeper ablaze.
Eyes on the horizon, I missed, almost,
the garter, run down mid-road.

Enticed by the warm dust,
slowed by the cooling air,
he's sunned his last on this earth.

I never see snakes, ex-lovers or ghosts.
It's just easier that way.

Today my terror caught me,
It was time.

I've vowed to see snakes.

It was simple, as if coil and curve,
the slither and sleek, sudden appearance
 of what we've loved or loathed
is a piece of a puzzle.

Or maybe just a turn in the road.
Just that.

By October's blood moon, the Hunter's moon,

I seek no elk,
nor wait in blinds, poised for winged presence.

I stalk nothing, am myself stalked
by what I've missed,
in leaves turning, what I have turned from.

The Consequences of Truth

Yesterday, sitting in a stream bed,
under old cottonwoods, earnestly shedding their bark,
their outspread leaves, girlish, quaking and torqued,
by the silky breeze of late summer.

We were far south, then,
not in our own place, where the morning
already smelled crisp, and us, gleeful custodians,
of rampant chamisa and bloomed aster.

I know something like a wing has broken inside me.
That part I have that knows to lift.
Whatever in me that takes part in the slippery, lit skin of creek.
A shaky sluice of light.

What casts the shadow, I wondered.
The darkness that makes and holds the real design.
I didn't know and still
don't know how I could sit
broken in such beauty.

Pulled

(after George Herbert)

Constant pine,

companion by day, as bed is made,
by night, star filled–
held on one branch, rosebreasted grosbeak,
and on another, an ancient pulley.

And so was pulled,
my restless heart from each to each.

Their balance perfect, all the rest swayed
into view and rested,

taut calibration:

but swift winged grief flew through,
and pulled me down, wrested me
to hang, between sky and ground.

Taught this equation, simple,
machine and bird, bird and machine,
The one that rises skyward, by desire and the other,
would bear us up by simple work.

Message in a Bottle

No letter yesterday,
nor one today.
And the glass pitcher of my longing has finally cracked,
water everywhere.

Today, while making tea,
I felt that tautness,
a string pulled tight between us,
my hands among the dishes.

Flowers bloomed
in the rooms in which I waited.

No answer, but echoes
in the tight bud of the lizardia,
the open skirts of lily.

This patience is my practice:
collecting and tending
vase and urn, bucket and cup
to hold the river of our meeting.

The Mesa the Shadow Built

There are very few landscapes as urgent as shadow,
though some can be traced on the smooth skin of apple.
That curve so like the picked clean bone
we found that day we walked the mesa.
Our last step, with horizon as doorway,
we walked into distance as if into delirium.

We were called into that delirium
by the slanting rays of steel gray shadow
that opened the sunlight into doorway
reminding us vaguely of the sheen on ripe apple,
a scent that followed us up on the mesa
creatures worrying a favored bone.

You're wondering if we found that bone,
or threw it down in our delirium.
But the Pedernal is not just any mesa,
and the light there isn't a skin to shadow
To paint or not is the question of apples
that turns a canvas into doorway.

It doesn't take a genius to recognize doorway.
Though it took O'Keeffe to see a bone.
Cezanne painted apple after apple,
producing a mountain and his own delirium.
All the while, light required shadow,
just as horizon demands a mesa.

Georgia demanded a mesa,
and walked through light as if a doorway
which is to say, she practiced seeing the shadow
that light has wrought inside bone.
The stillness she painted is the opposite of delirium
I mean it. It's a glamour of apple.

No, don't bother with apple.
Instead, head out and climb the mesa.
That is the journey that quiets delirium,
transforming darkness into doorway—
the way we know it in our bones,
the way we see the gleam in shadow.

Remember to taste shadow in autumn's first apple.
Drum moonlight with bone long abandoned to mesa,
that music, a doorway leading back from delirium.

Potato Longing

Small ruby, Peruvian purple, cream gold,
patient jewelry, struggling through caliche.

Our soil resistant
despite compost, and purchased topsoil.

Secretly, I discard clay clods.

When alone, I imagine the lettuce elsewhere.
Private salad, tomatoes where I want them.

I don't want my father to leave this world.

I plant this thought with the radishes,
the carrots, the beets.

This desire is the root of my garden.

My father's trustworthy absence,
a letter every so, a call.

Under impossible ground,
the presence of unseen eyes.

Thing in Itself

All angles this one,
sheen of desert lacquer
shows first, slip of slick skin,
then the lighter mocha of the inner.

Storm of small weight, potsy sized,
thrown for hopscotch, it will lie flat,
mark the spot to land on.

Licked first, licking found not flavor,
but the temperature of caves,
Tongue, an amazement of elevations.

Recorder stone, living another
unmetallic life on it's other face.
Landscape of dust and dung.

Turning and returning to the object at hand,

the mind moving towards stars and pulled to stones,
the mind in mind of stone,
exploding into dark constellations.

Object Lesson

Follow the dark,
the glister of down,
the beneath and metallic,
(light weight in your palm)
to your father, a direction, a cardinal point.

Follow that slight pressure.
Pointing, it indicates the place
where he is waiting, did always wait,
waits still.

A compression of emotion,
tonnage of sand, of seas,
pre-Cambrian love.

Tiny marker unearthed at my feet,
reminding me to go this way
towards that longing
we are at either end of.

Saying the Ridiculous

For the most anguished states of human consciousness,
psychology has merely developed a ridiculous vocabulary —Antonin Artaud

Ponderosa's have their own psychology,
revealed by spreading canopy and exposed roots.
It's a family secret, those resilient tendrils
sustaining a life of inconsistent water.

To be absolutely drenched,
isn't that what they long for?
The needs of trees are not ridiculous.

If I say I write to be loved,
I partly lie.
Those words run deep and have lived
from monsoon to monsoon.

I've pursued my heart's desire
in the small cottages of my poems.
But it wasn't what you might think.

There are certain farewells
we only say in rain.
Growing steadily wet,
some desires can wash off.

The longing that is left
is wet clay. Straw bound adobe
we build into a shelter, that too,
must give way in the storm.

Black Hollyhock, First Light

That spikey eye, dead center.

A practice of weeping.
A woman cries and cries,
leaning out of her body as if it was a window.

Becoming then,
a pillar of light,
a basket of leavened fire.

Salt, salt.

A flame,
blowing from storm to blossom
and back.

Too Many Bulbs in Autumn

I did it again. Bought and bought.

The truth is, by October,
I'm ready for it all to go away.

By first frost, I'm done.
I've had it with bud and bloom,
I'm ready for wilt and wane.

As usual, I've stuffed bulbs
in the mudroom's recesses,
along with other plans.

I take them out, tender and plump in their aereated bags.
Think, 3 inches deep, 5 inches apart,

I go out and scout the garden. It's full.
Of course.
It's always full in Fall.

Every year the catalogues come
in the full flush of summer,
when I am still in floral greed,

Huge allium and miniature daylilies,
new hybrid gladiolus, I won't have to dig and store.

Everything promises to naturalize.
Everything promises to fill my evening,
or mornings
with woozy scents and a stampede of blossoms,
riotous color.

I picture fields, acres, dappled in painstakingly
freewheeling color, absolutely Monet,
patterns of perfectly planned height and white giving way
to yellows to crimson, my own Sissinghurst,

Bluebells, I think, a meadow full, nodding in sleepy clusters
beneath the shade of pines. Foxgloves, and dahlias
big as dinner plates.

I mail in my pay nothing now postcards,
throwing caution and credit to the winds,

Then September, and the boxes arrive,
needing to be planted,
needing to be, at the very least, opened.

I can barely stand to see them.
I feel sick with guilt and glut.

Autumn crocuses, of all things.
What was I thinking?
Where did I think I would put them?

Of course! Back on the shelf!

Soon, I notice odd moonwhite shoots
from above the winter coats, peeping out from
single gloves and scarves we got as gifts.
Not possible, I think, don't even look.

Two days later, it's true.
Those ghostly white stalks have begun to open.

Today they bloomed, right where I'd hidden them.
Delicate translucent bells edged in mauve,
with vivid yellow stamen, an aroma like mortal sin.

We've gone way past gardening this year—
we are simply growing.

The Music of Canyon

Jibber jabber from above,
I struggle to fix the source.

Finally echolocate

tufted eared squirrel in the ponderosa's crown.

Early October, the long needles gone golden.

Who but the Stellar jays
know the ways of evergreens in Autumn?

What we least expect is turning.

We're ready for oak and ornamental plum,
but not this blush of pine along the ridge,
a secret kept by the deciduous ones.

I am bothered today, my neighbor starting
and stopping and running and starting
his generator all morning.

Trying to be poetic, Carmina Burana
through the sunny house,
but all this obstreperous music!

Just then the genny quits, a sudden silence
falls, broken only by thick, inconstant murmur
of wind, north south across the canyon.

The squirrel ceases his urgent chatter.
Magpie sipping in the still pond, stops,
only to have the chorus taken up afresh,

By a nectar drunk frenzy of wasps,
buzzed on the last dregs of summer's sugar water,
and a clan of nuthatchs, clicking beaks against bark.

The soprano soars, O Fortuna Imperatrix Mundi,
jet roars over, choral wind
brings the scent of bottomland upwards.

Surely there are many songs married here, this one,
quiet on the page, wet notes in slick ink, and these others,
sung through the canyon, in the key of falling needles.

Finally I See

60 miles we've traveled over aspen passes,
burning into winter.

Light flickers a jittery return
to the bones of the planet.

From within, the white bark glows.

Finally I see,
not the sun setting,

but the earth turning.

In No Musee at All, at All

How well the Chinese masters understood   hillsides
even in this century,   lyrical
calligraphy of mist, the careful
absence. Secret presence of rivers,   edge.

Even now. Even
today (bare birch on Connecticut hillside)
pine forest on silk scroll, suggests   hidden
water. Brushstrokes make the interior   gestures

Bare birch, what else? on Connecticut hillside,
Through trees, we print, or paint,   articulate
absence. Brushwork holds the spaces
that darken between pines. Silence enlarges   landscape.

We print or paint to articulate what we miss.
Rivers frame this language.
Silence frames this hillside.

On & On

Our lives make a right angle with the coffin.
We're always waiting
for everything to go well.

If there were a beginning and an end,
we could figure it out,
and leave it at that.

But really, each day adds a new mess to the heap,
here's laundry and there an unfinished thought,
not to mention the letters, or the kitchen.

Even the cat needs petting.
So much undone, even winter
has to go on and on. Just think of it,

light alit in ponderosa needles,
a wind sweeping east west through the canyon,
the next storm coming.

That Morning Thing

Sitting by the amaryllis
We gave into, impulse purchased, choosing "apple blossom"
Over the lurid red–

One tall foot high, sturdy,
The pot an irresistible setting for found rocks and marbles,
Errant seeds that sprout their spindly way to light.

Quiet, after so much rumpusing in dream:
Cars hurtling through air on purpose, I did it,
Don't ask.

A long section on the evolution of man,
The deconstruction of women
And the invention of the moon.

This time, an IBM Selectric flew by.
This time, the moon rose in an orangey haze
Over a midsummer pond.

This time it was full like nobody's business,
A 180 yr mysterium, throwing back solstice glow,
Showing a white, white throat to Deneb, Altair –

But now, no, that's poem and not astronomy,
Not lunar except in the way we say, "lunatic"
And mean ink on paper at 8:10 in the a.m.

Without which the day goes bad, and then the week,
And you've shot your whole life, a big zero,
Just by answering the phone, a question, or picking up socks.

Worthy activities, but fearsome, dangerous.
Think of that bud still folded in the amaryllis,
That might easily have stayed bulb.

(How does it happen, how did it happen?)
That it turns out I have bought this life, and filled it with soil
And curved bone, hummer feathers, and a slice of glaciated granite

Picked up the night the big, big moon rose
Over McAllister, after the snow geese
Had twisted the air into a tornado of music.

And we drove like fiends to see them settle,
And stand, us, not them, in the bitter blue cold,
On the prairie the Spanish named Llano Estacado, staked plains.

Which they had seen from the palisade of rock,
And it pleases me to write palisades,
Though I picture from across the Hudson,
The Jersey shore.

That tells you something about my rivers,
That names the explorer of my first stolen territories.
That is where I first saw moon ribbon on cold water.

And woke slowly, slowly, hoping to take up pen
And make slowly, slowly, a blossom
Come open in winter.

Lorca es Muerte, Despues

I am the stillness
a las cinco de la tarde.

In the sex department I am a goddess—
I know a hundreds ways to say: Maybe.

And I'm not afraid of the shadows of body parts
while they remain connected.

Telling lies to children is wrong.
As wrong as lambent sun in winter.

Make hay while your troubles shine.
We're having a blue light special on Happiness on aisle 4.

What would you give for melted brie on fresh pear?
What would you do for one true sentence?

A Ready Audience for Light

I was in a strange city.
I knew no one.
There were no voices in the close garden saying my name.
Under the gleam of pond, the bright glamour of Koi.

The koi were literate in light.
I was in a strange city.
The grasses were deep around my feet.
I knew the wind by name.

Pennies gleamed from the pebbled depths.
The koi read as light.
Such color is expensive.
The grasses grow deep around my heart.

From the clipped rhododendron, such a fabric of lit web,
Coppers gleamed from my own darkness.
Azaleas grow here and the commerce of making:
Such color is expensive.

The spiders traffic in private industry.
From the clipped rhododendron, a complexity knit in light.
Koi know the steps of the one who feeds them and their voice.
Azaleas grow here in public.

The light has moved to the further edge of pond.
The spiders know that darkness.

You can taste the commerce in a windy city.
Koi hear the step of the one that feeds them and their voice.

Koi grow fat on the industries of color.
The further edge of pond is a city.
Commerce traffics constantly in a web of light.
You could taste azaleas on the wind.

Velvet Sutra

for Robert Winson
Sei Gan Yo San

All being awake
is saying goodbye.

The shell opens, the meat
and sweetness devoured.

The Chinook blows.

Softly,
so we have no pride of emptiness.

Just vessel.

Vessel of sorrow
clear glass of parting

Sky night shining inside.

Water as full of light
as answers.

I Do, I Do

I pick up a gold ring from the floor
Belonging to no one I know.

I wed the absent, a piece of dust,
A drop of water.

Does this surprise you?

Think of me as a nun,
Marrying, unasked, the invisible.

Think of all confused God lovers
Whose eyes sparkle

Having lit on the shine

From the corner of a dark room.

Take It from the Top

Today I saw the secret heat of the rooted ones.
Snow fell late last night, leaving the ground
warm, brown & bare beneath the pines.

We woke to a peach fuzz fog, rolling down the canyon slopes,
and the canyon floor a creamy minted green.
Weather uproar! Red wing blackbirds calling the news tree to tree.

Finally, that hustering wind has calmed,
having made good on the promise of storm.
Such a glistering, glittering as spring re-arrives!

I feel like apologizing for loving pansies,
but they were my mother's favorite.
Here their monkey faces bloom crazy jubilant all winter.

Engorged with today's fresh wet,
the tissuey petals are tender, clairlucent.
What's not to love?

But the best is the snow gone to prisms of water
in the tree's needles. Budded with wet,
sending telegrams of color.

Writing a poem a day is difficult.
But if the world can start from scratch daily,
how hard is it to notice?

Cry Alpine

Long breath note of ridges

Sing that line, the peaks,
the long couloir.

You are there.
If only in song.

You can walk the erode and tumble in your own voice.

It's all about pitch.
And how you first knew sharp and flat.

Then you find that other, secret key.
Then you holler in bottom notes.

You are valley, you are ravine,
then the smaller, tighter places
between fallen logs
where everything grows.

colophon

Text set in *Deepdene*—
designed by Frederic W. Goudy in 1927
and named after his much-loved home and
studio/workshop near Marlborough, New York.
With its long & narrow serifs and angular stress,
the roman evokes an air & era of a thoughtful pen.
The italic remains one of his most distinctive and
made in the hope that "it would be found worthy
to stand alone, just as the older italics were
intended to stand." Combining the mellifluous
with vintage ruggedness, this fount achieves
a mien imbued with sensual levity
& a troubadour's golden wink.

•

Book design by J.B. Bryan

Judyth Hill writes from her studio at Rockmirth, near Las Vegas, New Mexico. She has published six previous books of poetry, incuding *Hardwired for Love* (Pennywhistle) and *Men Need Space* (Sherman Asher); founded the Chocolate Maven Bakery in Santa Fe; was director of TumbleWords for Western States Arts Federation; former coordinator of literary projects for New Mexico Arts; longtime ringleader of Talking Gourds; and well-known across the Colorado Plateau for her powerhouse readings. She has a cookbook *The Dharma of Baking*, forthcoming from Celestial Arts, and currently leads workshops around the country.